IT Management
MANAGING
PEOPLE

DAVID E McKEAN

About the Author and IT Leaders

DAVID MCKEAN IS A FORMER CIO WHO HAS WORKED FOR SEVERAL MULTINATIONAL COMPANIES AROUND THE WORLD, INCLUDING AT&T subsidiaries in Asia, UPC Nederland in Holland, and C&W UK. Through his work with IT Leaders, he has worked alongside some of the top IT managers and CIOs from around the world. Through these experiences, he began to understand why some IT professionals make it, and others don't.

IT Leaders runs public courses, distance-learning programs, blended learning, and in-house courses. Public courses on IT business management and IT leadership are conducted regularly at Henley on Thames, UK; New York City, US; Dubai, UAE; and Singapore. All IT Leaders programs are accredited by the Institute of Leadership and Management, and they are presented by former CIOs and senior-level directors.

Delegates include IT managers from companies all over the world and of every size and industry. Our clients include Accenture, Allen & Overy, Alstom, Amey, Barclays, Boeing, BT, Capita, Debenhams, DHL, HP, HSBC, John Laing, Philips, Rothschild, Royal Bank of Canada, and Siemens.

The IT Leaders program looks at eight key IT leadership skills, including organizational politics for IT managers; leading IT teams; business and IT strategy; technology innovation; crisis leadership; business change leadership; senior level influencing; and corporate leadership.

The IT management and commercial excellence program topics include IT to business alignment; business relationship management; managing IT teams; technology sourcing; negotiation' and finance for IT managers.

The blended and distance learning programs are available worldwide and are based on the ten management skills model developed by IT Leaders. Courses are live and interactive, using online seminars, e-learning, and assignments backed by a comprehensive course guide and mentoring from the course leader.

IT Leaders also runs a vibrant network of IT managers, open to former delegates and all other IT managers for a small annual subscription. The network group is vendor-independent and meets three times a year at Henley on Thames in Oxfordshire and online to listen to top leadership and management presenters, as well as to discuss key topics of interest.

This book is based on the experiences of our delegates and additional interviewees. If you have any comments or management learning that you would like to be considered for future editions, please feel free to e-mail me at david.mckean@itleaders.co.uk.

Contents

The Secret to Good IT Management

THIS BOOK IS BASED ON THE EXPERIENCES OF A LARGE NUMBER OF SENIOR IT MANAGERS AND PRESENTS THEIR GUIDELINES FOR SUCcess. If you are expecting large models and great analysis, you may be a bit disappointed, but bear with us. The skills that will make the biggest difference to your personal success are the ones we describe here.

The development of IT management skills presents a constant dilemma. Most IT managers are promoted from a technical position that relied on technical skills, yet these skills count for very little in their new management job. Many managers respond by "keeping their hand in"— in other words, interfering. They get frustrated because they perceive themselves to be less valuable than they were before. They feel as if they have been chosen for the swimming team, because they were once good at tennis.

In fact, _successful_ IT management boils down to some fundamental, but quite small, differences. Understanding these differences helps to identify why some IT professionals make it and others don't. This book gives you this inside track directly from the experiences of others, revealing their secrets to good IT management together with some tools and techniques to aid you. My aim is to help you maximize your skills in these areas, so you can fulfill your true potential.

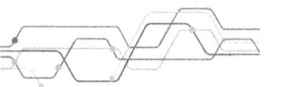

BEN'S STORY: WHAT NOW BOSS?

I remember vividly my first job as an IT director. I was working for a large organization in Cape Town, South Africa. I had arrived at my hotel at 2 a.m. after a long flight. My management team, seeking to impress me with their enthusiasm, had arranged to meet me at 8 a.m. the following morning.

I looked at them through bloodshot eyes, as they asked eagerly, "What should we do now, boss?" It was a seminal moment for me. The plain truth was that I had no idea. The people around the table knew a lot more than I did. As I found out later, new managers often have this feeling of being out of their depth, of feeling like a bit of a fraud. In truth, no new manager can ever possibly know everything from the outset. Fortunately, in my case, I stumbled through by asking a number of smart questions, and I used the experience of the team to guide me.

When asking IT managers "What do you want to know when it comes to IT management?" the most commone response is "What do we need to do?" But compiling a long list of IT activities doesn't—on its own—make for good IT management. Yes, an IT organization needs to plan, implement, and operate the information systems for an organization to meet its objectives. But the real question is: What exactly should I do to make my IT organization excel versus another?

To answer this, let's think about the key objectives of IT management, which fall broadly into three categories:

1. Plan the information systems strategy and technology architecture to meet the needs of the business. Good IT strategy needs to take into account the priorities of the business. Good technology architecture needs to take into account new and existing technologies and identify suitable opportunities where they may be able to help the business.

2. Implement IT projects that enable the business to improve its efficiency, reduce costs, and deliver a competitive advantage. A key success

factors is close cooperation with the business leaders to understand their requirements and set priorities. It also requires good governance, risk management, and working closely with the business sponsors to address the people issues associated with major change programs.

3. Operate information systems so that they are fast, scalable, reliable, and secure. They need to be user-friendly and available to those who need them. There should be good processes in place to enable users to log problems and have them quickly resolved.

Although techniques for good planning, implementation, and operations are the building blocks of successful IT management, first and foremost, successful IT management is about people, building and running IT teams, managing project sponsors, and working closely with users to ensure their needs are met.

This book is the first of four in a series on IT management, and it focuses on the people side of IT management. Other books in the series will cover IT management skills for planning; implementation; and operational performance, respectively. The outline of the books in the series is shown in table 1.

Book 1: Managing People	Book 2: IT Strategy and Technology Innovation
Managing yourself Managing IT teams Managing business relationships Working with senior execs	Business strategy IT strategy Technology innovation IT governance
Book 3: Managing IT Projects and Leading Change	Book 4: Business Management and Operational Performance
Project and program management Risk management Leading business change Project portfolio management	Technology sourcing and negotiation Finance for IT managers Operational excellence Crisis handling and problem solving

TABLE 1 - THE IT MANAGEMENT SERIES

It was striking that all the CIOs interviewed for this book were avid readers. Throughout the footnotes of this book, you will find references to some excellent books that have been a source of inspiration to many.

This book is first and foremost a practical guide based on real experience. I hope it will give you some new ideas and inspire you to do things differently.

1. What Makes a Successful IT Manager?

1.1 EMOTIONAL INTELLIGENCE

Companies have been preoccupied for years with trying to understand the most important leadership skills that deliver the best business results. In the 1990s, Daniel Goleman[1] wrote a paper called "What Makes a Leader?" He worked with many organizations to find out which managers were considered their best leaders. His work was based on the business results of those managers and the opinions of their peers. The research identified five key skills, namely **self-awareness, self-regulation, motivation, empathy,** and **social skill,** which he collectively called "emotional intelligence."

This list really resonates with many IT managers. When IT managers were asked to identify what distinguished the best bosses they had ever worked for, the answers included being a good listener, having a good sense of humor (actually the most common response), being trustworthy, being knowledgeable, and so on. All of these are directly attributable to emotional intelligence.

---

1   Daniel Goleman, "What Makes a Leader?," *Harvard Business Review* (1998).

DAVID'S STORY: IN A GOOD MOOD

As it happened, shortly after I read the paper on emotional intelligence, I was given a stark reminder of the importance of self-awareness. I was busily working at my desk and looked up to see a queue forming outside my door. There were about five of my managers and other team members waiting in line to see me. Thinking that something was up, I asked my assistant what had caused this sudden rush of interest. She looked a little embarrassed, but eventually revealed that she had sent a note out to the department, saying that I was "in a good mood" and that if any of them needed a favor (such as signing expenses), now might be a good time. This certainly made me smile (I really *was* in a good mood!), but as I reflected, it occurred to me that my own impression of myself was not how others saw me. I had no idea that I had such "good days" and "bad days." My self-awareness needed some work.

If you have not read Goleman's paper, I would urge you to do so. Three of the five characteristics— self-awareness, self-regulation, and motivation—are to do with what we call personal leadership, which is the ability to manage yourself.

Recognizing one's strengths and weaknesses (self-awareness) is vital. Managers who are self-aware know where they are going. They set targets for themselves that—although difficult and challenging—are achievable. In turn, this track record of achievement gives them a self-confidence that rubs off on others. These managers are usually very honest people, guided by a set of personal principles. If you interview someone with high self-awareness, they will be able to tell you what their shortcomings are, and also have strategies in place to overcome them.

Self-awareness comes from noticing the effect that we have on the things around us. Usually, the signs are there if we look for them.

Sometimes, they may need pointing out. If you look back on the best bosses you have ever worked for, you will probably see that they were the ones who honestly told you what you were good at and what you needed to work on.

A good way to understand strengths and weaknesses is to do a 360-degree survey. This is when your manager, your peers, your direct reports, and end users or customers are asked to comment on your strengths and weaknesses. There are several methods in place to assist with these surveys. We work with the Hay 360 emotional competency inventory (www.haygroup.com), for example, which is based on Goleman's emotional intelligence model.

Another assessment that you can easily carry out is called *Strengths Finder 2.0*[2]. This book, by Tom Rath, contains a code and a link to do the test online. It will identify your top five key strengths, which reflects a changing attitude to leadership thinking. In the past, doing things better meant working on weaknesses. If we do have significant weaknesses (for example, poor delegation skills), then it is important to work on them. In summary, though, we should play to our strengths.

1.2 IT MANAGEMENT STYLES

In our leadership course, we ask delegates to complete a psychometric questionnaire, which helps them to understand what sort of manager they are in terms of their style of communication. This assessment can be life-changing for some managers. They start to learn that managers behave in completely different ways, even when presented with the exact same scenario. Every manager has a natural, preferred way of communicating that is a fundamental part of their character. As managers progress in their careers, they become more versatile in adapting to different methods, but fundamentally, their natural, preferred style never changes.

---

2   Tom Rath, *Strengths Finder 2.0*, (Washington, DC: Gallup Press, 2007).

Think about which one you inherently adhere to. The four styles of communication are:

Logical and structured: We have now assessed over one thousand IT managers. Not surprisingly, over 60 percent of IT managers fall into this category. These are people who like a lot of factual detail. They like the facts to be presented in a structured and logical order.	**High level thinkers:** Studies suggest that approximately 70 percent of chief executives fall into this category and probably about 20 percent of IT managers. These people like information at a high level. They are easily bored and hate a lot of details.
Friendly: These are sociable people who live very much in the here and now. This type makes up 30 percent of the general population, but less than 5 percent of IT managers. They tend to be exceptional managers of people. They take time to talk informally about all sorts of things before getting down to business.	**Creative types:** Creative people think in terms of pictures and images. They are visionaries who see the future clearly. Often eloquent and artistic, they value relationships and can see possibilities for the future. About 15 percent of IT managers fall into this group.

FIGURE 1. LEADERSHIP AND COMMUNICATION STYLES

Knowing our natural communication style is very important, particularly when working with other styles—which is normally the case. Your position in figure 1 determines how you relate to other managers. If you are not clear on which is your style, you could be facing the wrong way—in other words, communicating in the wrong style. We discuss this in more detail in chapter 5.

Self-regulation is the other side of self-awareness. There is no point knowing what your weaknesses are if you don't do anything about them. Self-regulation is about regulating your emotions and keeping a balanced view of things. It means staying calm when someone comes to tell you that the payroll system has crashed, for example; or a key project needs to be delayed. Managers with good self-regulation are able to get to the heart of problems and ask key questions in a composed way.

Where self-regulated managers are more able to adjust to difficult situations, the reverse is also true. Managers who do not stay calm when presented with bad news will soon discover that no one tells them what is going on. Self-regulation can also be about putting strategies in place to overcome weaknesses. So, a manager who is (self) aware that he or she does not present well when rushed always takes the time to prepare properly. Self-regulation is that little voice inside you, talking through the different options and suggesting which one might work best in a particular situation.

The third personal characteristic of emotional intelligence is motivation. Managers with high motivation are always looking for ways to do things better. They never take "no" for an answer, although they usually won't take on the impossible. They like to keep score, so they can see positive progress.

JIM'S STORY: WHERE THERE'S A WILL

Jim was head of operations for a large organization in Indonesia. The company's main data center was out of date and needed replacing. Jim designed the layout and specified the equipment required. It turned out that all the equipment could be delivered within a few weeks, with the exception of the server racks.

These would take several months, and that assumed no problems with customs. Rather than delay the plan, he drafted up a design with pencil and paper and set off to find a machine shop. After some searching, he found a company that was able to work to his drawings, and they handcrafted the racks in four weeks. A world-class data center was completed in just three months. Jim showed an extraordinary level of motivation. While others around him were already changing the completion date on the project plan, Jim was looking for a different way.

1.3 SUCCESSFUL CIO BEHAVIORS

Organizational hierarchies in today's world are much flatter than they were, say, thirty years ago. This should be applauded, but even within this new egalitarian society, managers are still expected to display different behaviors than their staff. In table 2, you will find a list of what

to do—and what *not* to do—to get ahead. The list was compiled by a leading headhunter, and it is based on her experience of working with top CEOs.

Impressing the CEO at the Interview	
THINGS TO DO:	**THINGS NOT TO DO**
1. Convey complex concepts in an interesting and clear way. Senior managers don't want drawn-out descriptions. They want to know what the technology can do for them.	1. Talk endlessly about technology.
	2. Be blissfully unaware of one's shortcomings. When asked about their weaknesses, poor candidates often say something like "I suppose I sometimes work too hard," or "I don't suffer fools gladly." Better to have something a bit more interesting to say (although stay away from admissions of embezzlement!)
2. Express yourself powerfully and be able to answer questions thoughtfully and without too much detail, getting your point across clearly and persuasively.	
3. Demonstrate exceptional influencing skills, recognizing that different people are influenced by different things and influenced in different ways.	3. Go for any job: Managers should be discerning about which opportunities they apply for and do their homework.
4. Be engaging and interesting with a sense of humor. Show an interest in new things and a thirst for knowledge.	4. Dress badly: IT executives should dress like their colleagues in other parts of the business. Ill-fitting suits and hair that appears to have been cut with a knife and fork give a bad impression. Interestingly, in a straw poll of HR managers, over 50 percent said they pay attention to a candidate's shoes.
5. Be part of the inner sanctum: In every organization, there is a small group of five or six top managers who informally make all of the key decisions of the company. It includes the CEO, CFO, and generally two or three others. Not being aware of such a group is a sure sign that you are not part of this group and not influencing things at the highest level.	5. Blame the business: The business "couldn't make up their minds" or "we had to educate the users in our new processes." Both of these patronizing phrases instantly suggest someone who does not respect or work closely with the user community.

TABLE 2. IMPRESSING THE CIO AT INTERVIEW

Let us focus on four behaviors in particular:

Dress correctly: Whether you like it or not, first impressions basically come down to appearance—dress, haircut, shoes, accessories, and so on. Most people will tell you that their first impressions tend to be accurate. Even if they aren't, it will be quite some time before they change them. It was interesting that over half the CIOs we interviewed mentioned the issue of dress without being prompted. All of them were wearing suits, and more than half were wearing ties.

A senior manager who is considering someone for a promotion will want him to demonstrate that he can already do the job. The hiring manager will ask herself: "Can I see this person in that job, in that chair?" Vintage t-shirts and nose piercings, for example, are just not helpful.

Communicate well: Clear and concise language is vital—no mumbling, rambling, losing the thread of conversation, or talking too much. Written communication should be clear and polite. One way to test this, by the way, is to look at your e-mail "sent items." You will find the answer there. And what about spelling? Many top managers I've worked with were terrible spellers, but they always used spell check and asked people around them to quietly make any necessary corrections. Spelling may not be the same as management ability, but it is distracting.

Even the way a manager answers the phone is important. It is vital to return calls, get back to people, and deliver on commitments. Any single item weighted on its own may not be that important, but add them all together, and you have your behavior.

Make it interesting: Having good conversational skills is very important. Being knowledgeable about your company or organization makes you interesting to your peers. Read the business press to find out what is happening in the marketplace and look at your company's website on a regular basis to keep up-to-date on new product launches, financial results, and so on. And take time to understand new technology trends, so you can explain them clearly to others.

Be streetwise: Many managers go about their business completely oblivious to the risks and consequences of what they are doing. We are not talking about financial risks. We are talking about career risks. These managers take on new projects without consideration as to what is needed and whether they have enough control to make things happen.

Let us take the example of top athletes. Contrary to popular belief, they do not take on just any challenge. They set achievable goals for themselves. When they master those goals, they look for the next one. They follow a guided path in what is called the Competition Zone or "C Zone."[3] They do not stay with one activity so long that it becomes boring—avoiding the so-called "drone zone." Equally, they avoid taking on challenges that are too difficult and lead them into the "panic zone." Over time, as their confidence and skills increase, they are able to take on greater and greater challenges. So, they are never out of control, and they never take something on without thinking.

1.4 WHERE SUCCESSFUL IT MANAGERS SPEND TIME

1.4.1 Busy Fools

When I ask managers how many e-mails they get a day, answers usually range from thirty to over one hundred. Those at the higher end are generally proud of this, and in some cases, e-mail completely defines their job and—to be honest—usually their lives. Often, though, these are the very same managers that don't receive the recognition they deserve. For these managers, it is clear that they need to work smarter and avoid being "busy fools."

Ironically, time management is often one of the first management courses that managers attend. Guidelines generally include how to stop procrastinating, handle things only once, group items together for when

---

3   Robert Kriegel and Marilyn Kriegel, *The Competition Zone: Peak Performance Under Pressure* (New York: Ballantine Books, 1994).

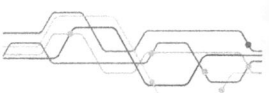

you call someone, and so on; in summary, how to get more done in a day. In amongst all these, there are two golden rules for IT managers:

- Have the right things on your list. As per the old adage, managers do things right, and leaders do the right things,

- Do them in order of priority, making sure the big tasks fit into your calendar first. Think of your calendar as a fish tank with only so much space. Your large priority tasks are like rocks. You need to put these big rocks in your calendar first, and then spread the pebbles and sand (i.e., smaller tasks) around them. This is the best way to make the most out of your available time

1.4.2 Urgent or Important?

So the first question is, "Which tasks should make it to the priority list?" To do this, we need to categorize our tasks. Every activity has two key characteristics. The first is its urgency—in other words, does it need to be done immediately, soon, or sometime in the future? The second is importance. Is it of high, medium, or low importance? Plotting these variables on a Boston matrix creates four possible combinations, which are labeled with a quadrant number in figure 2. A task can therefore be:

- Quadrant 1—Urgent and important. This includes key reporting requirements, regular meetings, resolving immediate technical issues, crisis response, and so on.

- Quadrant 2—Important, but not urgent. This includes longer-term activities, such as IT strategy, crisis planning, problem prevention, team building, and personal development.

- Quadrant 3—Urgent, but not important. This includes less-important meetings and lower-priority e-mail and calls.

- Quadrant 4—Neither urgent nor important. This includes filing and administration activities, amongst other things.

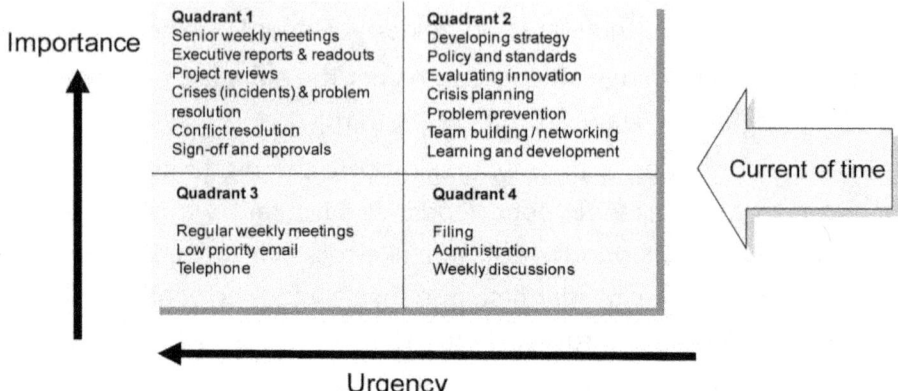

FIGURE 2. URGENT VS. IMPORTANT

How you categorize a task is entirely up to you. What is important to you may not be to someone else, although hopefully your boss will agree with your assessment.

All managers need to spend time in quadrant 1 (urgent and important). It is just a question of how much. Although most managers think that they should be spending more time in quadrant 1 than any other, the research tells us otherwise[4]. **The most effective managers spend more time in quadrant 2** (important, but not yet urgent) compared to their less-effective colleagues.

---

4   Steven R. Covey, *The 7 Habits of Highly Effective People*, (2004).

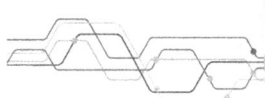

THE STORY OF LEO & MICHAEL

Our research has found that there are only small differences between successful and less-successful managers. To illustrate this, we put together a DVD [5](available at www.itleaders.co.uk). It tells a story of two IT managers who run similar organizations and have a similar day ahead of them. As we track their progress, we see that Leo (the leader) is well-prepared and working in quadrant 2. Michael (the manager) is less prepared, spending a lot of time on detailed technical activities, always under time pressure and much less effective.

The punch line though, is that both managers were played by television actor, David Gillespie. David could transform immediately from one character to another with a change of clothes and a change of what actors call "status," the characteristic that defines a person's confidence, or lack of it. Actors are highly skilled at playing with status. The point is that many people who watch the video do not realize at first that it is the same person. Only small changes are needed to make a completely different impression.

What does this tell us? Simply put, the way to be effective is to address important tasks early, before they become urgent. To take a technical example, a task that might be "important but not urgent" today—such as storage capacity planning—might suddenly translate into an urgent and important task when the disks are full. And a task that might have required a half day to put into place ahead of time, if neglected, might now demand a week of several people's time.

There is effectively a current of time moving from the right to the left on figure 2. So, if you sit on something that is not due until next week, it will drift from being not urgent today on the right-hand side of the

5   IT Leaders, "Leadership Time: the Story of Leo & Michael," (Oxfordshire, United Kingdom: IT Leaders, 2009), DVD.

matrix to becoming urgent on the left-hand side next week. Managers who do not recognize the importance of doing things ahead of time find themselves constantly fighting fires. This increases stress levels and reduces performance. (Perhaps you know some managers who fall into this category.)

Activities in quadrant 2 are often, but not always, leadership-type activities. They are typically larger in scope and usually involve other people—either team members or peers around the organization. They include business and IT strategy, high-level governance, problem prevention, and your own private goals.

Quadrant 2 tasks make the biggest difference to your performance and effectiveness.

Some managers will need to spend more time in quadrant 1 than others, due to the nature of their work. For example, incident desk managers will generally be involved with calls from users who have a problem right now, rather than sometime next week. These managers will still need to dedicate time to quadrant 2 activities, such as root-cause analysis, to reduce the number of repeat calls. One organization we worked with found that over 15 percent of calls to the incident desk were for password resets. Some pre-planning would have easily identified that the password format was too complicated.

Quadrant 3 tasks—the ones that are urgent, but not important—often include routine weekly meetings, lower-priority e-mails, and so on. ("Not important" should really be called "less important," as it is unlikely that an activity is completely unnecessary.) Think about how to achieve the same outcome in less time. For example, a weekly meeting might be very helpful, but if it could be done in thirty minutes rather than an hour, the time spent on a per-minute basis would make it twice as important.

Quadrant 4 activities are the "neither urgent nor important" tasks, such as the worst of e-mail. Examples might include weekly news bulletins that are full of advertisements masquerading as stories, spending too much time smartening up a presentation, or creating a long report that no one reads. Don't confuse "not important" with "boring." Team members who don't complete their expenses on time, for example, should organize themselves better.

1.5 CHANGING YOUR TIME PROFILE

There is nothing more important (or obvious) to achieving career success than changing where your time is spent. Here are five steps to improving your time management.

1. **Write down your business and personal objectives.** Some of these will come from your personal development plan; others you should add in yourself, particularly around personal development. Use the form on the next page to list your thoughts.

2. **Look at your current activities.** Work out how much time you spend on each one. Plot them on the urgent vs. important matrix, using a relative scale with respect to their objectives. There is no value putting everything in quadrant 1 or quadrant 2. Your "less-important" tasks should be in quadrant 3 or 4.

3. **Retain key activities.** Highlight activities that are a key part of your job and need to be retained; for example, the delivery of projects, operational management, budget management, and so on.

4. **Out with the old.** If improving performance means changing what you do, you will need to free up some time before adding anything new. (Unless, of course, you are not very busy at the moment.) Look through your calendar and e-mail, and put together a list of the ten least-important or most time-consuming things you do. You now have four options as to how to deal with them:
   - Delete them: Things that are not important at all should be stopped immediately.

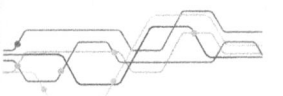

- Delegate them: Pass them to someone else, not necessarily someone working for you.
- Do them better: For example, if you have a two-hour project review meeting, think about how you could complete it in one hour or even a half-hour.
- Defer them; In other words, identify activities that aren't such a priority. Be careful not to defer quadrant 2 activities, though.

5. **In with the new.** Highlight some new areas to emphasize. These will include your own ideas to change your quadrant 1/quadrant 2 balance, plus some new leadership opportunities. Our research suggests that leadership opportunities for IT managers fall into one of ten categories, as shown in figure 3. To help you along, there is a list of leadership opportunities for "Leading People" in Chapter 5. For the other three categories, you will have to read the other books in this series. This list has been compiled over a period of time from IT managers in all industries working around the world.

Leading people	Leading change	Leading performance	Leading business
Personal leadership Setting and achieving goals and aspirations	**Strategic leadership** Developing IT strategy & business alignment	**Operational excellence** Fostering a culture of continuous improvement	**Business management** Enhancing business management skills
Team leadership Managing & inspiring technology teams	**Thought leadership** Using technology to bring about innovation	**Crisis leadership** Handling serious incidents	**Corporate leadership** Guiding the business at the highest level
Peer leadership Building influence with other business managers	**Change leadership** Guiding the business to deliver business change		

FIGURE 3. LEADERSHIP SKILLS AND AREAS OF OPPORTUNITY

Collect Your Thoughts

Use the form below to improve your time profile. Start with your objectives and your important tasks today. Put together a list of things to stop or do less of. Add some new quadrant 2—or leadership—opportunities.

	Five Key Objectives	
	Five Important Things You Do	
	Five Things to Stop or Reduce	
	Five New Things	

TABLE 3. COLLECT YOUR THOUGHTS

1.6 MAKE YOUR CHANGES COUNT

For an objective to really succeed, it needs some careful thought. It needs a "well-formed outcome," a technique that comes from the world of neurolinguistic programming (NLP)[6]. The idea is to think carefully about the desired outcome of an objective. From this, we can put some steps in place to achieve what we really want.

There are six stages that need to be followed :

1. State your desired outcome in a positive way. For example, let us suppose that we are smokers, and we want to give up. Just saying that we want to give up is not sufficient. We need to get to the heart of *why* we want to give up. The outcome needs to be stated in positive terms; for example, "We want to get fit, because we want to climb Mount Kilimanjaro next year."

2. Next, think about if this is going to be a win-win for everyone. So, to take our "quit smoking" example, there is no point going off to the gym every night for training, and leaving our partners at home with the children. So we need to say something like, "We are going to get fit enough to climb Mount Kilimanjaro by going swimming every Tuesday and running early every Saturday."

3. The third part of the well-formed outcome is that it needs to fit with who we are. There is no point going swimming every Tuesday if we can't swim or running early on Saturday if we don't like getting up early.

4. Next, think about the necessary steps. Going swimming once a week and running once a week is a good start. But will it get us fit enough? The fitness activity at the beginning is an important first step, but we may need other steps, too.

5. A well-formed outcome also needs to be self-maintained. To take a trivial example, if we are reliant on someone driving us to the

6   Sue Knight, *NLP at Work, the Essence of Excellence*, (2009).

swimming pool on Tuesdays, and they are not always available, it won't be long before we fall out of the routine, and any benefit is lost.

6. And finally, our well-formed outcome needs to be something we are willing to pay the price for. Yes, it would be great to climb Mount Kilimanjaro, but if we really don't want to stop smoking, go swimming, give up sleeping in on Saturdays, or pay for an expensive trip, then we need to think of a different outcome.

This simple process encourages you to think about the desired outcome. And by working through how to get there, it makes it much more likely to be achieved. Think about how you could apply the "well-formed outcome" thinking to your key business and personal objectives.

2. Team Leadership

In this chapter, we discuss what makes a good IT team. The objective is to help you think about how you currently run your team and offer some new ideas. As an IT manager, you probably already recognize that leading technology teams requires particular skills and expertise. Technology teams have their own characteristics. For example, most IT team members are highly trained, and often have a technical degree. But strongly developed, highly logical minds can also create their own problems! IT employees often believe that technical knowledge is of the utmost importance and a very good measure of ability. And they are sometimes surprised to see how highly companies value employees who have limited technical understanding.

IT people are often self-sufficient, which can reduce the communication among team members. They also love solving problems, and they are often on the lookout for problems to solve. Unfortunately, this can appear very negative to outsiders. Observations of IT staff also suggest that they may find it difficult to work in a hierarchical organization and to take instruction, particularly if their managers are not technical. Team managers, therefore, need to be more inclusive in their approach; think carefully about how work is allocated; and recognize the importance of good technical skills.

In summary, there are some real differences in the makeup of technology teams compared to other company departments. In the next nine sections, we discuss our top guidelines for managing IT teams.

2.1 RECRUIT GOOD PEOPLE

The team you inherit won't be perfect—but that's all the more reason to make the most of any opportunity that presents itself to improve your team. Take these opportunities wisely, and follow these guidelines:

- If possible, ask for the right to hire one or two people onto your team when you take the job. Ideally, you should be looking to bring in people with whom you've worked in the past.

- If you do need to hire from outside, and you do not have a candidate readily available, choose a good recruitment firm or headhunter. Work with them to choose the best candidates. Pay attention to the style, layout, and ordering of their CVs. It tells you a lot about the candidates; how they view themselves and their achievements. Look at more, rather than fewer, CVs. It will take you only one minute to scan a CV, if you know what you are looking for. Recruitment opportunities are too important to waste.

- Be clear what you are asking for, but don't be too specific. The skills you need today may well change in a few weeks. You may regret it if you choose a specialist who can't adapt. Good people will be versatile.

- Always conduct your interviews with a colleague; ideally, your HR manager. It will serve you well in terms of speeding things up, getting a second opinion on candidates, and keeping you tuned in to a group that generally knows everything that is going on. HR will understand the procedural side of interviewing, as well as the legal aspects, such as age, sex, and racial discrimination laws. They will probably have a better understanding of market pay rates, as well. In short, they will help you find better people, quicker.

- Think about what competencies are required for the role. "Competency interviews" are used quite frequently these days. Here, every interview is conducted in the same way with the same questions to test for specific competencies required for the job. When you are recruiting technical people, make sure their technical knowledge is thoroughly tested (i.e., don't take their word that they are competent, just because they did it in their last job.) All the major blue chip companies that I work with require candidates to take a written test whenever technical knowledge is required. Remember that competence is not the same as personality, so make sure you test for that, too. Research shows that "gut feel" can also be a valuable tool[7] in choosing the right candidate. One IT director we work with asks one of his team to take any potential candidate out for lunch. The team member can tell him a lot about how the candidate would fit in.

- Prepare properly for interviewing candidates. There is nothing more certain to put off qualified candidates than an interviewer who doesn't know their name or hasn't read their CV. Less-qualified candidates will not be put off, so lack of preparation is the best way to ensure that you get lower-level candidates.

- Put candidates at ease—you are recruiting them to do a job in the IT department, not to be good in high-pressure interviews. Ask them what they know about your company, and listen carefully to their answer. Of course, knowing about your company isn't the same as being able to do the job, but at least you will know if they want it. There is no greater mistake than recruiting someone who can do the job, but doesn't want to.

- As the interviewer, take care not to talk too much in the interview. Studies show that interviewers rate candidates higher in proportion to how much the interviewer talks, so take care not to be misled by someone who managed to keep you talking, but is not suitable.

- It can take time to find the right people. Don't be tempted to give in to deadlines. If you are in doubt, keep looking. It is important to get the right people on board. It would be a terrible shame if to fill a rare vacancy with the wrong person.

---

7   Malcolm Gladwell, *Blink*, (2006).

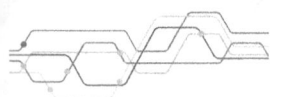

2.2 IT ORGANIZATION

2.2.1 Organizational Structures

Good organization for the overall IT department is vital. Many options and permutations exist and include the following, or, indeed, a combination of the following:

- Life cycle (e.g., strategy and planning, projects, application support, infrastructure)
- Process (e.g., sales process, manufacturing process)
- Departmental (e.g., sales department, distribution)
- Location (e.g., Europe, Asia, North America)
- Application (e.g., ERP, CRM)

The ideal structure depends on the topology of the company, but a structure with a department each for planning, projects, and infrastructure, plus application support mirroring the business units, is usually a good starting point. Set up your reporting lines carefully. Typically, a manager will have between five and nine reports. Recognize that there is no perfect solution, and the most difficult problems need to be placed with your best managers.

Think about the flow of information among your team members. Each overlap is a potential opportunity that they will need to come to you for resolution. If possible, put people with similar skill sets in the same areas to help with resource allocation. Keep the project list manageable to keep the department working effectively. Give consideration to how the organization appears to the rest of the business. Points of contact should be clear, and if your business relationship managers promise something to the business users, they should have the authority to deliver it.

2.2.2 Clear Roles and Responsibilities

A key part of organizational management is the development of the right skills and deploying them to best effect. The Skills Framework for the

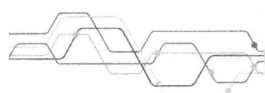

Information Age (SFIA)[8] provides a clear, universally recognized model for describing an IT practitioner's skills. They are defined in two axes:

- **Categories**—which are further broken down into subcategories to group standard IT job roles
- **Levels**—which define the different levels of competence or attainment

SFIA does not define the categories or subcategories. It defines only the skills. The categories and subcategories are merely a way of organizing the skills on paper. So, the categories and subcategories might change according to your organization. Clearly, there are also behavioral skills (which some people refer to as "soft skills"), but SFIA deals with what we refer to as "professional skills."

SFIA Categories
Strategy and architecture
Business change
Solution development and implementation
Service management
Procurement and management support
Client interface

SFIA Levels
7. Set strategy/inspire, mobilize
6. Initiate/influence
5. Ensure/advise
4. Enable
3. Apply
2. Assist
1. Follow

TABLES 4A AND 4B. SFIA CATEGORIES AND LEVELS

The resulting matrix of these two axes shows the complete set of skills used by IT practitioners. SFIA provides an overall description for each skill, supported by a description of how the skill appears at each level of competency at which it is recognized. A skill does not normally appear at all seven levels.

---

8   "Skills Framework for the Information Age (SFIA)," www.sfia.org.uk. SFIA is the intellectual property of the SFIA Foundation, a not-for-profit organization that distributes SFIA free of charge to end users.

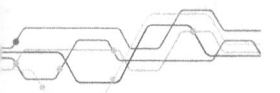

2.3 CREATE HARMONY

Top teams work together in a particular and distinct way and normally have a set of team values to guide them. Value statements reflect the actual beliefs of an organization and must be backed up with actions, so there is clear evidence that they are supported. They guide behavior and, in effect, define culture. For a team to work in harmony, this code is vital. There are five characteristics of particular importance for successful teambuilding.

Mutual respect: This refers how people in the company interact with each other and the respect they show for everyone at all levels. In France, the tradition of shaking hands with your colleagues each morning is a great example that reinforces communication and demonstrates mutual respect. The military has long had a tradition of getting together briefly at eleven o'clock every morning for coffee. These rituals emphasize the core beliefs of mutual respect.

PLACES WHERE PEOPLE COULDN'T SAY WHAT THEY THOUGHT

In his book, *How NASA Builds Teams*,[9] Charlie Pellerin tells the story of the Hubble telescope. At the time, he was NASA's director of astrophysics. Although the launch was successful, it soon became apparent that there was a serious flaw in the mirror. Sometime later, the failure review board told Congress that the flawed mirror was down to a leadership problem. It transpired that the contractors had not forwarded the results of numerous tests, which might have identified the failings. When asked why not, they reported that they were "tired of the beatings." NASA had become so hostile to its contractors that they stopped reporting any technical problems.

---

9   Charles J. Pellerin, *How NASA Builds Teams*, (2009).

Malcolm Gladwell, in his book *Outliers*,[10] tells the story of Korean Air, whose planes in the early 1990s were crashing at a rate seventeen times that of the industry average. In a typical accident, there are seven consecutive human errors. These are rarely errors of technical or flying know-how, but errors of teamwork and communication. Investigators found that the captain's social status was so high that the junior officers could only communicate obliquely and deferentially. In one case, the captain was trying to land the plane in severe weather conditions. He had committed to a visual approach, and the navigator knew there was worse weather ahead. Rather than clearly state that they were heading into a highly dangerous situation with no backup plan, he said, "The radar can help us a lot." The captain was tired and not listening to the hidden meaning. Ten minutes later, the plane crashed.

Honesty and trust: Lencioni,[11] in his work on dysfunctional teams, emphasized the importance of trust in a team. He showed how teams without trust get sucked into a downward spiral of mistrust and poor performance. One of the greatest forces in creating distrust is when the organization is in competition with itself, with similar functions divided across departments. The good news, though, is that if you spot such a problem early, re-organizing the fragmented functions often transforms teams very quickly. IT managers need to build the positive circle of trust. Trust breeds cooperation, which in turn breeds commitment, accountability, and attention to results. This increases trust, and so the spiral of trust becomes a self-fulfilling prophesy.

Pride and a sense of belonging: This is shown in how a company works together and the emphasis it places on teamwork; for example, the importance of keeping commitments and supporting other team members.

10   Malcolm Gladwell, *Outliers: the Story of Success*, (2009).
11   Patrick Lencioni, *The Five Dysfunctions of a Team*, (2002).

Many organizations foster a sense of belonging through their values and often a dress code. For example, some companies have a special company uniform, whereas others are more relaxed with "casual Fridays." These codes represent the culture of a company; what works for one company may not work for another.

Commitment and loyalty: Any successful company must to foster pride in hard work to remain successful, and at the heart of this is the commitment to the customer. Leading customer care is the job of everyone, not just those in direct contact with the customer. Objectives need to be set that make sure everyone shares in the company's commitment to quality and customer care.

Attitude to risk-taking: An organization needs to know where it stands in terms of innovation and risk. Is it conservative, or does it like to cutting edge? It is all very well for a company to say they encourage risk-taking and innovation. The test comes when something goes wrong—does the management team stay supportive?

International Teams: Diplomatic Relations

In today's IT world, more and more teams are international in nature. Understanding the different outlooks of different cultures is an increasingly vital skill for IT managers. In collaboration with a number of international CIOs, we have put together this list of six guidelines for working across international and cultural boundaries.

1. **Be easy to understand**. For those of you who are native or fluent English speakers, you are fortunate that English is international language of business. But even though it is second nature for you, be patient with those who are not natural English speakers. It is important that you speak clearly, which generally also means slowly. Use short sentences and simple grammatical structures, and avoid long words and slang expressions.

2. **Write down important instructions**. One technique that worked well for the CIO of a large technology company was to write detailed e-mails, explaining instructions and providing guidance for key activities at critical times. E-mail allows words to be fine-tuned, making the meaning clear and unambiguous. Colleagues can also refer back to it.

3. **Really take time to listen**. I mean, really listen. It may mean long pauses in the conversation while colleagues are trying to find the right words to express themselves. You should never attempt to finish someone's sentence. Pay attention to make sure you are not interrupting.

4. **Recognize that your way isn't necessarily right**. And it certainly isn't the only way. Different countries approach problems in different ways. Just because something worked for you in your country doesn't mean it will work in another. Never underestimate the resourcefulness, intelligence, and expertise of the people you are working with. Seek to find the middle ground; in other words, take time to think of ideas that capture the best of everything from both sides—methods, experience, and cultures. Indonesians have an expression, *gatong rayong*, which literally means "carrying together," and reflects the importance of colleagues working together on plans that they have all signed up to.

5. **Be sensitive to culture and social context**. One of the most exciting and rewarding aspects of working in an international environment is the opportunity to learn about other cultures. Be sensitive to the fact that different cultures value different things. For example, so-called "high context" cultures, such as China and Korea, place a very high value on experience and seniority. Showing respect is essential in these environments. Always seek to learn about the way things are done. Be sensitive to everything and everyone around you, and adjust your behavior accordingly.

6. **Not all good news is good news**. Be aware that you may appear threatening to other cultures for any number of reasons. Show humility, and encourage your colleagues to come forward with problems without fear of criticism or reprimand. Many cultures do not like to give bad news and can—shall we say—distort the real truth. A soft approach, demonstrating trustworthiness, is essential.

TABLE 5. DIPLOMATIC RELATIONS: GUIDELINES FOR INTERNATIONAL TEAMS

2.4 CREATING A BALANCE OF SKILLS

It is important to hire good people with the right skills, but this alone will not guarantee success. We also need to try and ensure that our team has the right balance of skills, so it can portray the right behaviors. To use the analogy of football or hockey, you would not want a team where everyone wants to be scoring goals—you need everyone to work closely together and divide up all of the work. Dr. Meredith Belbin[12] conducted extensive research on the subject of teams and developed a simple and practical model.

His research identified that every successful team needs skills in nine areas, and that someone should fill each of these nine roles or functions, or problems will occur. Since many teams have less than nine members, team members will often fulfill more than one role. However, unlike a

---

12   Meredith Belbin, *Team Roles at Work*, (2010).

psychometric profile, it is relatively easy to take on a different role if cir-
cumstances require. To assess your team roles, go to the Belbin website at
www.belbin.com. For a relatively small cost, you can complete the online
survey, for yourself or, better still, for your whole team. There is also some
free resource material to accompany the team role tests.

The Nine Belbin Roles

PLANT: Creative, imaginative, and unorthodox. Solves difficult problems.

RESOURCE INVESTIGATOR: Extroverted, enthusiastic, and communicative. Explores
opportunities. Develops contacts.

COORDINATOR: Mature, confident, and trusting. A good chairperson. Clarifies goals,
promotes decision making.

SHAPER: Dynamic, outgoing, and high-strung. Challenges, pressurizes, finds ways around
obstacles. Reviews progress of the project, and gives energy/re-direction as necessary.

MONITOR/EVALUATOR: Sober, strategic, and discerning. Sees all options and has a
reputation for making accurate judgments.

TEAM WORKERS: Sociable, perceptive, and accommodating. Listens to what is going
on and can sense when things are not right. Good diplomats and can avert difficult
situations.

IMPLEMENTER: Disciplined, reliable, conservative, and efficient. Turns ideas into
practical action.

COMPLETER/FINISHER: Painstaking, conscientious, and often anxious. Searches out
errors and omissions, and makes sure the project delivers a good level of quality.

SPECIALIST: Single-minded, self-starting, and dedicated. Provides knowledge or
technical skills that are in rare supply.

TABLE 6. BELBIN ROLES

Team members generally fulfill their roles at all times, but some really
come into their own during particular stages of a project. At the outset, a
project needs the ideas person—the plant in Belbin terms. Of course, not all
ideas are good ideas, so the monitor/evaluator is needed to select the best
ones. Once the project is under way, you need a project manager, usually
fulfilled by the coordinator, and someone to find the resources—the resource
investigator. Next, the work of the implementer and team worker begins,

and the project makes progress. From time to time, it will be necessary for the shaper to look at things from a high level and re-direct the project if required. As the project nears completion, the skills of the completer/finisher come into play to ensure that the product is delivered to a high standard of quality.

It is important to have expertise in different roles. Celebrate diversity in your team. Teams with lots of implementers implement lots of projects, but not necessarily the right ones. We often find lots of implementers and quite a few shapers amongst IT managers, but—it has to be said—not many plants.

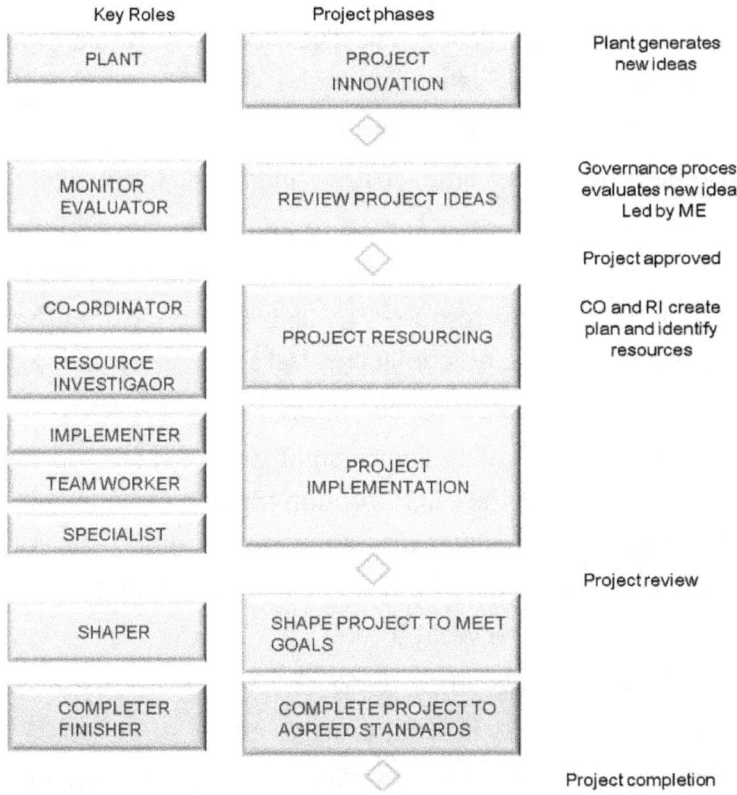

FIGURE 4. THE CHANGING EMPHASIS OF ROLES IN A PROJECT

2.5 SET DIRECTION AND OBJECTIVES

Good direction and clear objectives have a massive positive effect on the success of any team. Estimates suggest that performance can be increased by

20 percent with good, well-thought-through targets. Management books talk about vision as being an essential ingredient, and so it is. But vision also needs some reality sprinkled in, particularly for IT people. IT strategy should describe both your vision and the actual targets you are seeking to achieve.

As described by Kaplan and Norton[13] in their book *The Balanced Scorecard*, objectives should be set in each of the four quadrants of the balanced scorecard, namely, customer or end-user objectives (in the case of IT); process objectives, including technical performance (again, in the case of IT case); people objectives; and financial objectives.

From the IT objectives, define objectives for every IT team member. Objectives should be properly defined using the SMART acronym, as follows:

- **S**pecific—clearly defined and unambiguous
- **M**easurable—in terms of time, cost, quantity, and/or quality
- **A**chievable—in other words, agreed to and understood by the team member
- **R**ealistic—the necessary resources available, enough time has been allocated, and there are no conflicting tasks
- **T**imely—a clear timetable is agreed upon

All objectives should have a line of sight, where there is a clear link from the top-level goals of the CEO, through the departmental objectives of IT, to the individual objectives of every team member. The following three questions will help assess if a team has good direction:

1. Does the team know what to do?
2. Does the team know when to do it?
3. Does the team know in what order to do it?

Objectives should have both a baseline—which is the minimum level to be achieved—and a stretch target. Stretch targets can be an enormous source of motivation, allowing team members to prove that they can do more than just their job description.

---

13   Kaplan and Norton, *The Balanced Scorecard, Translating Strategy into Action* (1996).

2.6 CREATE GOOD WORKING CONDITIONS

The more we've worked with IT teams, the more we've come to realize the importance of a good office environment. No two companies are the same, and what works for one may not work for another. Yet too few IT departments think carefully about what is required, or what could be improved. Office space is particularly important for IT staff, as they are more likely to be doing their work at their desks, rather than out on the road, visiting customers, for example. Break-out areas, where teams can discuss issues spontaneously, are vital.

AHMED'S STORY: WHERE HAVE ALL MY STAFF GONE?

I was working in a hospital, running a team of IT staff. We had been based in a new annex, but it was undergoing some renovation. In the meantime, we were moved back to the main building, into the basement. It was just like a scene out of the TV program *The IT Crowd*. There was no natural light, and the corridors were used as a storage area. The whole mood of the team changed. We lost 30 percent of our staff in six months.

As their manager, I thought my job was to keep them motivated and persuade them to stay. It was only after four or five months that I realized I was putting my energy in the wrong place. I should have been fighting for better conditions, not appeasing my staff. I spoke to the CEO and found us two temporary locations above ground. It was still another six months before we moved back to our original refurbished office, but at least we didn't lose any more staff. It made me realize that you *can* change your working conditions if you put your mind to it, and your team will really respect you as a result.

The working environment includes many things, such as:

- location and access of the office to public transport or parking;
- location relative to other departments, for example, in the same building or on the same campus;

- the quality of the office decor, including furniture, and other office facilities, such as printers and copiers;
- working conditions, such as air conditioning and lighting;
- a proper reception area and enough meeting rooms;
- and additional facilities, such as break-out areas, quiet rooms, vending machines, cafeterias, and gyms.

Changing the working environment really does make a major difference to productivity. Think about your working environment. It is easy to think that it is the responsibility of the facilities manager or someone else, but it is surprising what you can achieve with a little application.

Finally, the rest of the organization is looking to you to create good, easy-to-use IT. Some of this comes down to ergonomics and the physical environment. IT managers should work with HR to make sure that screens are well-maintained and large enough for the task, attention is given to prevention of RSI (repetitive strain injuries) with good design, laptops are easily portable, and chairs are comfortable. Options such as thin client desktop computers are ideal for reducing office noise—it is easy to forget how noisy work environments can become.

2.7 DEVELOPING SKILLS

In the world of IT, it is important to keep abreast of new technical developments and keep skills relevant. IT managers have a duty to develop their team. Here are some ideas that will help.

2.7.1 Delegate and Coach

All managers need to delegate to get their job done. But the way in which managers delegate says a lot about their effectiveness. It also provides a great opportunity for developing team skills. Use different styles in different situations[14]. For example, for new, inexperienced team members, act as a teacher, providing clear instructions for what needs to be done and how

---

14   Hersey, Blanchard, and Johnson, *Management & Organizational Behaviour*, (1996).

to best go about doing it. For more-experienced team members, act as their coach. Outline what needs to b e done, and guide them to the right approach. For experienced managers, give a high-level view of what is required, and make yourself available to act as a sounding board if needed.

Coaching is not a simple exercise, but it can be a highly effective way to develop the skills of your team. It can be done formally, through regular progress reviews, or informally, taking advantage of opportunities in the day-to-day working environment. This book is too short to discuss coaching in depth, but I have found the book *Masterful Coaching*[15] helpful.

Six Steps to Giving Good Feedback

Good feedback is at the heart of managing employee performance, but it is easier said than done. It is not the same as praise, and certainly not the same as criticism. It is a regular discussion of performance, recognizing what went well and what could be improved. Managers who give regular feedback find that it is a strong source of continuous improvement and motivation. The process we recommend here has six stages:

1. Be clear in your own mind what it is that needs improving, with an outline view as to how this may be achieved. Prepare this before speaking to the team member, or you risk being either vague or inaccurate.

2. Identify a suitable opportunity to give the feedback, and ask permission before you go ahead. Choosing the right opportunity is very important—there is nothing worse than the manager who pops his head around the door and says, "Can I have a word, please?" This strikes fear into the heart of most people, and it will reduce the likelihood of the feedback having a positive result.

3. Once agreement has been given for a feedback discussion, give an example of what was said or done (or, sometimes, not done).

4. Explain the impact that you thought this had, and give a balanced view to maintain rapport. Listen carefully to the team member's view.

5. Assuming that your feedback is considered valid by the team member, reach an agreement on what needs to change; in other words, commit to what needs to stop, start, or continue.

6. Finally, get an acknowledgement that the team member is happy with the feedback and has taken it on board. This keeps the channels open for future feedback discussions.

TABLE 7. SIX STEPS TO GIVING GOOD FEEDBACK

---

15   Hargrove, *Masterful Coaching*, (2008).

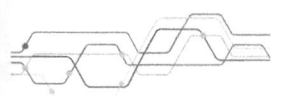

2.7.2 Team Meetings

Regular IT team meetings are the ideal opportunity to develop skills. To avoid overlap with day-to-day issues, schedule a half day of development every two or three months. Allocate the time early, and choose the topics. Consider inviting the managing director to talk about plans for the future or the marketing director to talk about new products, for example. Alternatively, ask a team member, industry expert, or external training company to run the session. Make them interactive—listening to presentations for four hours rarely makes for an interesting or productive afternoon.

2.7.3 Business Meetings

Normal business meetings are also a great way to develop team skills. If one of your team members is running the meeting, spend ten minutes or so with them beforehand to get them to think about what the meeting is for and the desired outcomes. Ask them what role they would like you to play, and identify a couple of development areas to focus on. Typical objectives you may set might include:

- Building rapport: looking for ways outside the meeting to get to know peers and senior managers better.
- Building influence: for example, with a key sponsor or business user.
- Understanding problems better: for example, using advanced questioning techniques.
- Finding out what is happening in the organization: learning more about products, senior-level strategy, and such.

Working with your team members on a one-to-one basis, such as this, helps in many other ways. You will develop your unspoken set of rules and better manage the discussions. For example, while one asks the questions, the other can be listening carefully and preparing questions to find out more.

2.7.4 Training Courses

An obvious way to develop IT management and technical skills quickly is through a training program. For example, my company, IT Leaders,

runs accredited public, in-house, and distance learning for IT management and leadership. Other companies offer IT process training, such as PRINCE II, ITIL, and more technical courses.

2.7.5 Use Vendors and Networks

Leading vendors offer an excellent insight into the IT industry. They work for many organizations at a time, and they know the market and the latest technology intimately. Many produce white papers and journal articles. They know what the future of the industry will bring, because they are already working on the next generation of products. It is worth asking your account managers to bring in their senior architects and marketing directors to update you on the latest trends and innovations.

External consultants can also help to develop skills. If you are about to commission a new consulting assignment, allocate one of your IT team members to the consulting team to retain the knowledge in-house. Examples of such assignments might include developing strategic plans, creating a manual of IT standards, or evaluating supplier spending.

2.7.6 Networking

There are many networking groups set up for IT managers, including our own IT Leaders Network, which meets three times a year. Networking is not just about joining network groups. It is important for all IT managers to build a close group of peers, associates, and colleagues who they can confide in. This is easier said than done, and it takes time and a concerted, proactive effort to achieve.

2.8 MANAGING PERFORMANCE

It may take time to find out whether someone is simply in the wrong job, or whether their career is best served elsewhere. If you have a problem with one of your people, it may be helpful to review how it came about. Be aware, though, that most problems are down to management. To assess if this is the case for you, ask the following three questions:

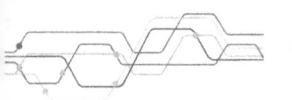

- Does the team member have the skills they need to do the job and, if not, why not? Is it a problem with recruitment, or are they in a role that doesn't suit them?
- Is their poor performance down to external factors (e.g., personal problems), or an attitude tarnished by previous bad management?
- Are they doing an impossible task? Perhaps the job is undoable because of inadequate resources or the wrong contractors. Is it caused by a root problem with procurement, perhaps?

If you know you need to make a staff change, then act quickly. Be tough and focused. Notify HR at the earliest opportunity, and don't stop until the problem is resolved.

DIETER'S STORY: ACT NOW WITH DISRUPTIVE PEOPLE

I had just joined a new company as the IT director. I soon found out that one of my direct reports had also applied for the job, but of course had not been successful. This person became very disruptive, and was increasingly causing problems with the other managers. I chose to work with him for several weeks before the situation came to a head, and an agreement was made for him to leave.

It was not that he was a bad person—just one in the wrong position. Once he had gone, the whole dynamic and productivity of the department transformed. It reminded me of when a car alarm goes off down the road. You don't realize how annoying it is until it stops. At first, I thought it would be too much hassle to sort it out, but, looking back, it would have been better all-around if I had acted more quickly.

It is much easier to recruit good, high-quality people than to invest a lot of time in those who will never make the grade. This sounds harsh, but we shouldn't forget the fact that poor performers are usually unhappy

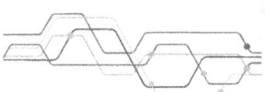

and unfulfilled in their work, and it often suits everyone to find them something else to do. A poorly performing employee can really damage team morale and productivity. Jim Collins describes in his book *Good to Great*[16] that great companies still "churn" (i.e. turn over) as many people as less-successful companies. Churn is defined as staff turnover from employees moving to new jobs, retiring, or being fired (i.e., not from layoffs). It wasn't that they churned more or less; they churned better. So people either stayed a long time, or left sooner.

2.9 REWARDS AND RECOGNITION

Our final guideline for building strong teams pertains to rewards, in particular, rewarding the right behavior and matching actions to consequences. The process starts with the manager asking a team member to carry out a particular activity. Instinctively, the team member will want to know what is in it for him—what are the positive and negative consequences, and how can he influence those consequences?

Interestingly, actions and consequences often contradict each other. For example, you would expect that if a particular activity was performed well, there would be positive consequences for this. And similarly, if the activity was not performed well, there would be negative consequences. But in fact, we often see that positive actions have negative consequences, and negative actions have positive ones.

A good example came from the customer care department of one of our clients. One incident manager was particularly good at handling difficult, awkward, and sometimes rude customers. So you can probably guess that the reward that he got for his skill was to spend all day handling difficult customers. If we do not give consideration to the link between the action and its consequence, we can unwittingly demoralize our team.

Finally, if your team has been successful, you need a way to celebrate. Team celebrations can sometimes be met with a groan from cynical team

---

16   Jim Collins, *Good to Great*, (2001).

members, so care should be taken to do it in the right way. As we have said, technology teams can be different, and they may not see a reception—accompanied by a load of strangers—as reward for anything. But if done in the right way, team celebrations are good opportunities to acknowledge the great work that a team has done, inspiring it to continue and grow. Rewards cover a wide range from a simple thank-you to a job promotion, and everything in between. Examples, in no particular order, might include:

- Dinner for employees and their partners
- Pay raises and on-the-spot awards
- Team awards
- 'Freebies,' such as T-shirts, thumb drives, and so on
- A research budget to try out new technologies

3. Business Relationship Management

3.1 BUILDING RAPPORT AND CREDIBILITY

Business relationship management is a key responsibility of every IT manager. It is important to project the right image to the right people. Many IT managers think managing the relationship side is quite difficult. Often, working in a technical environment offers limited exposure to working with other managers. But it is not impossible; it just needs practice.

IAN'S STORY: WHAT'S ON YOUR MIND?

I was the head of business relationship management for our Canadian division based in Montreal, having just moved from our US headquarters. I had been part of the design team that put together a corporate architecture using best-in-breed applications around an integration layer. It was a pretty neat solution, and we were keen for the Canadian subsidiary to adopt it.

Unfortunately, they didn't see things our way. As a recently acquired division, the business sponsors told me they were happy with what they had and didn't want some fancy (read: expensive) head office solution. The meetings became pretty heated.

Jennifer had just joined the company as the Canadian head of IT. What she did at the first meeting was amazing. Instead of talking about the US architecture, she asked them about their problems. What was keeping them up at night?

As it turned out, quite a lot! She asked about the implications of this, in terms of revenue lost, cost savings missed, quality, and so on. Before we knew it, they were starting to talk about the importance of replacing parts of the existing systems. Within a few months, some of the old systems had been replaced completely with modules from the new architecture. In fact, all the systems were replaced within just eighteen months.

Over a quiet drink one evening, Jennifer confided in me that she had used a technique called SPIN, originally developed by Neil Rackham for the world of sales. The essence is to focus on user problems and their full business impact. It taught me a lot, especially how much we can learn from sales when working in business relationship management.

First of all, have something to say. Comedians often say that it takes a lot of practice to be spontaneous. So, do as they do, and prepare your lines beforehand. Like them, you may not know exactly what you are going to say, but the conversation will give prompts to something you have thought about already. Think about subjects of interest and common ground.

Be observant. See who gets recognized and what they talk about. Keep on the lookout for opportunities to help. Be consistently polite and return phone calls, answer e-mails, and meet deadlines. In short, keep your commitments. Don't whine to your co-workers about what is wrong. Bounce ideas around with them as to what a good solution might be. And, finally, treat every discussion with the business managers as an opportunity not to be missed.

Building rapport with business managers is the first step. But to get things done, every manager needs credibility. With credibility comes opportunity, and with opportunity comes success. Credibility is a key leadership attribute. It is the heart of business, and it is its most valuable weapon. Without it, failure is guaranteed. Credibility means that others believe and trust what you are saying, and consequently seek your opinion. Credibility is subjective in nature, but table 8 shows our seven guidelines for building credibility with your peers.

Credibility Guidelines
1.   Know your own company organization and the people you work with.
2.   Have good sources of information, and quote them when appropriate.
3.   Build a good track record.
4.   Discuss concerns directly with people involved.
5.   Be professional and speak calmly, accurately, and concisely.
6.   Ask insightful questions and encourage a response.
7.   Listen to what people are saying.

TABLE 8. CREDIBILITY GUIDELINES

3.2 UNDERSTANDING CLIENT PRIORITIES

A vital aspect of business relationship management is understanding the priorities of business units and distinguishing between what is essential—"the needs"—and what is helpful (but not essential)—"the wants." Sometimes IT managers hear the word "want" and assume it means "frivolous." It doesn't. Just because something is a "want" doesn't mean it isn't valuable. Imagine being given a smart phone today that doesn't do e-mail. Well, e-mail isn't *essential* on a phone, after all—you have your PC for that! Emotional forces are often contained within the "want list," and delivering them may provide much-needed energy and support to get a project completed.

A technique used for understanding wants and needs is called "chunking up," a rather inelegant expression that means asking the business sponsors and users about their priorities and trying to get to the

heart of what they really want. It tries to get behind the *feature* of what is desired (e.g., a large screen), in order to understand the underlying *benefit* (e.g., it's easier to see, which means they can work longer, which means they are more valuable to the company, and so on). The technique often repeats the key question "Why?" in different forms; so, in our example, we might have asked, "So what does that do?" or "What will that get you?" and "How does that help?" to get to the real benefit of the original request for a large screen.

Richard Mullender—Police Hostage Negotiator

At one of our recent IT networking events, we were fortunate to have invited a former police hostage negotiator, Richard Mullender. As someone who handled life-or-death situations every day of his working life, it is no surprise that his questioning and listening skills were extraordinary. He kindly gave us some insight into the most important communication skill, a process called *active listening*.

1. Use "minimal encouragers." These are the little words that we can use to keep people talking, such as "And?" or "Go on."

2. Summarize—this gives the other party a chance to say whether he agrees, or more likely, add further background.

3. Highlight and echo energy words—for example, "We really need this for March." Here, if you hear them emphasizing "March," then it means it is probably the main energy word. If you just echo this by saying, "For March?" the likelihood is the other party will tell you why.

4. Mirror their posture which makes you more like them. The more you are like them, the more they like you.

5. Label understanding—interpret in your own words what you heard them say. For example:
    - I feel as if...
    - I sense that...
    - It appears to me that...
    - It sounds to me like...
    - It seems to me that...

6. Listen from their point of view—not autobiographic, silent, combative, or conciliatory—but from their point of view.

From Richard Mullender, Cliff Edge Communications

TABLE 9. ACTIVE LISTENING

Guiding conversations with business sponsors is a vital skill for any business relationship manager. The use of smart questions is a hugely versatile technique. Here are some different types of questions to use at different times in your discussions.

1. Most people are familiar with open questions. These are ones that require an answer of more than one word. They are helpful in getting the other party talking. Examples might include, "What are the implications of this?" or "Do you have any suggestions as to how we might improve this for next time?"

2. The opposite of the open question is, logically enough, the closed question. This is when you are looking for a one-word answer. These are useful to get absolute clarity about the truth. For example, "Do you think this will be ready on Tuesday?" You often see journalists trying to pin down politicians with closed questions, demanding a single word response; for example, "Were you, or were you not, aware that this was going on?"

3. Probing questions are the next level up, and they require a certain amount of skill and sophistication. They invariably build upon the answer from a previous question that provides an opportunity to ask a secondary question. In effect, they are used to try to find out more about a particular situation.

4. Multiple questions are also helpful. This is where you ask two or more questions in one. Although this may sound confusing, the effect it has is quite interesting. The person replying hears multiple questions, and usually interprets it as a request to tell you everything they know about a particular situation. It can be very successful in uncovering hidden information. Oddly, it is very rare that respondents answer the multiple questions clearly and succinctly in the order they were asked.

5. Leading questions are famously used by lawyers to get people to admit something they might not otherwise do. An example might be, "Is it not true that you knew you would not be able to meet the delivery times when we placed the order?" Leading questions are often

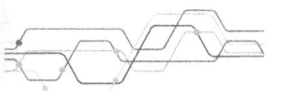

closed questions, as they request a one-word answer, but rarely get one.

6. Reflective questions are helpful to calm a meeting down. It might be a way to summarize a situation. For example, "It seems to me that we are going to have to delay this project unless the equipment is delivered earlier." At first glance, this looks like a statement, but you are asking the other party to respond, and either agree or explain why this isn't the case.

7. Finally, we have hypothetical questions. These are very useful tools for the negotiator. Also known as "what if" questions, these are good for exploring possibilities and suggesting possible trade-offs. For example, "What if we were able to give a two-year commitment; do you think you would be able to reduce your prices by 10 percent?"

Good questions	Good listening skills
1. What can I do to help you?	1. Focus on the other person, and don't be distracted,
2. Can you explain the process?	2. Listen from their point of view.
3. How do you feel about it?	3. Work with their agenda, not yours.
4. Can you explain that further?	4. See the other person as a friend, not a threat.
5. What does everybody think?	5. Given them time to finish. Don't be afraid of silence.
6. What can we change to make this better?	6. Let their answers guide your questions.
7. What key results are we looking for?	7. Listen carefully to what they have to say.
8. What do we think went wrong?	8. Write notes to show you are paying attention.
9. What are the implications of this?	9. Be enthusiastic.
10. What has to be done?	10. Practice your active listening.

TABLE 10. GOOD QUESTIONING AND LISTENING

Always take a trusted colleague with you, so you can work together. It can be very difficult to formulate a question accurately at the same time you are listening to the nuances of an answer. Having a partner allows each of you to think around the situation while the other is asking questions. Good questioning and listening skills are the keys to gaining a proper understanding of your customers' requirements and priorities— feel free to use them as often as you can.

3.3 HANDLING OBJECTIONS AND GAINING COMMITMENT

When we suggest something—for example, how we might implement a new project—we may find that our sponsors are not in agreement. They may have several objections to the ideas put forward. Typical objection-type questions might be:

- Why will it take so long?
- Why is this so expensive?
- How come my fourteen-year-old son can create a database in an afternoon, and yet it takes you more than two months and half a million dollars?

If you are programed to react the wrong way; then react the wrong way you will. In other words, if you see objections as negative, then you will see the above statements as negative. But they are perfectly reasonable questions, particularly if—as in the example above—the project is expensive and going to take quite a long time. These objections are, in fact, merely a request for more information. Far from being negative, objections are usually a positive sign and provide the perfect opportunity to address valid concerns. Sales executives will tell you that when a prospective customer has no objections or comments to a proposal, it usually means that they are not interested and won't buy.

So, to return to the example above, when the business sponsor asked the question about lead time, she may not have been aware that the user experts wouldn't be available for three weeks, or that new functionality was added in at the last minute, requiring a completely different system configuration. So what is the best way to approach objections? Our top seven tips for handling objections are:

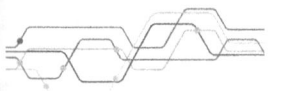

1. Try and handle them in advance—in other words, before the main meeting.

2. Take time to listen to the requirement. Don't argue or interrupt.

3. Think carefully about why this situation might be different for this client.

4. Keep discussing options (together).

5. Ask what other options they would consider or, indeed, have considered.

6. Talk about how others clients have felt in similar situations and what they found.

7. Recognize an objection might just be a grouse. "Why will it take so long?" might just be a negotiation ploy to see if you can deliver it earlier, but it does not necessarily mean that you have to.

So let us assume that all the objections have been overcome in a mutually agreeable way. What happens next? Well, if you were a salesperson, you would instinctively ask for the order…what is known in sales parlance known as "closing the sale." Salespeople have historically been very interested in this, not least because it is the stage before they receive their commission check. It is where they get the **commitment** to go ahead with the order. Table 11 gives some examples of useful techniques for obtaining commitment from users and business sponsors.

Techniques for Getting Commitment

- **Be assumptive**—This is when you believe your business sponsor has made up her mind to go ahead. You can say something like, "Shall we draw up the business plan, then, and present it together at the capital committee meeting?"
- **"Sounds to me"**—This is where you say something like, 'It sounds to me as though you are happy to go ahead and…"
- **"Two alternatives"**—This is one of the most common techniques used by salespeople. It gives the customer the choice between two options. "Do you want to go ahead with solution A or solution B?"

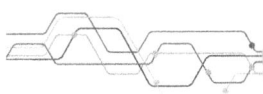

- **"Standing room only"**—"We need to close the books on this one, as our development resource is almost fully committed for the next three months with project Y."
- **"Last chance"—This is telling your customer that you need to move ahead with this, as you understand the vendor is increasing its prices next month.**

TABLE 11. TECHNIQUES FOR GAINING COMMITMENT

Closing is a really valuable tool that every IT manager must master. It is the most effective way to get a commitment from your business sponsors and users. Closing techniques should be used to gain incrementally smaller commitments. As stated earlier, timing is everything, and the commitment requested has to be reasonably in line with the discussion. Step-by-step commitments lead naturally to the final agreement. If the IT manager doesn't do this, a lot of work can be done without the agreement of the user or sponsor. At any time, they can turn around and say, "This is not what we wanted."

Think about using these closing guidelines in your meetings. Sometimes it is helpful to ask for a commitment, even when you know you won't get it. For example, you may be discussing the scope of a low-priority project that is drifting on. You might ask something like, "Would you be happy if we started work on a prototype for this?" fully expecting the reply, "Well, I don't think we are ready yet. My team is tied up on other things." Since this is what you suspected, you can now suggest, "Why don't we put it on hold then, for the time being?" knowing that it will probably never resurface. Clearly, it is better to focus your attention on what the customer really wants than it is to spread yourself across too many projects.

4. Working with Senior Execs—Networking and Politics

4.1 NETWORKING IN GENERAL

Effective networking is one of the most important leadership skills that every IT manager must develop. Research shows that the more senior the manager, the more time he or she tends to spend on networking. In fact, one study conducted by Dr. Robina Chatham estimated that some managers spend up to 50 percent of their time on it. This high percentage was recognition that these managers viewed many activities as peer leadership, including anything from short discussions to regular meetings.

JANE'S STORY: "DO AS YOU ARE TOLD"

I had often noticed that some of my managers took up a lot more of my time than others. But I had never wondered what my boss thought of me from this point of view. I had heard, though, that good leaders can become difficult followers without realizing it.

For me, it started when I was given responsibility for a new group of project managers in Eastern Europe. They were scattered far and wide. I was stretched to the limit and kept taking up more of my boss's time in asking for advice. My boss was getting frustrated with me, because I kept arguing against her suggestions. Looking back, I should have just done as I was told!

Apparently, there comes a "tipping point" when employees earn a bad reputation. Once past this point, it becomes a self-fulfilling prophesy where they get blamed for everything. I suspect that I was approaching this point. Luckily, I averted disaster by recruiting someone to take over the department, but still report to me. It taught me the importance of being easy to manage—in other words, to keep a handle on when and how often I spoke to my boss and what we discussed. Now I think about the problem in advance, present a couple of options to talk through, and better listen to the advice I am asking for.

Networking is very closely coupled to political influence and power. Politics, and in particular office politics, has some very bad connotations. We aim to dispel some of these myths and make it easy for you to understand what needs to be done and how to achieve it.

4.2 SOME FACTS OF LIFE BEFORE YOU START

So before we go on, let's talk about a couple of facts of organizational life.

1. Fairness is an impossible goal. Organizations are not democracies, and not everyone gets a chance to vote. Part of the job of influencing is to make things unfair in your favor.

2. Manage your boss—your boss is important to the business and important to you. You may or may not like your boss, but you need to be clear in understanding that he or she has enormous influence over you and your success. Your boss can help you succeed in other parts of the organization. Keep him or her fully informed of your actions and make your boss aware of your achievements. Support your boss; even compliment him or her from time to time. Ask what is on his or her mind, and take an interest in his or her priorities.

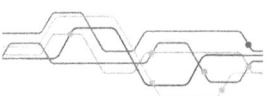

Senior managers tend to behave differently and usually need to be handled differently. Here are some guidelines for dealing with senior executives.

Don't ever tell them they can't do something. It'll just make them cross, and they'll do it anyhow. Isabella was the head of customer care for a technology firm in Sweden. She was told by the IT department that it wouldn't be possible to implement a new customer care scripting module. It was particularly important for new customer care representatives to be able to handle calls soon after joining. So she hired some programmers and did it herself. It was professionally done and highly effective. The IT department looked unresponsive as a result.

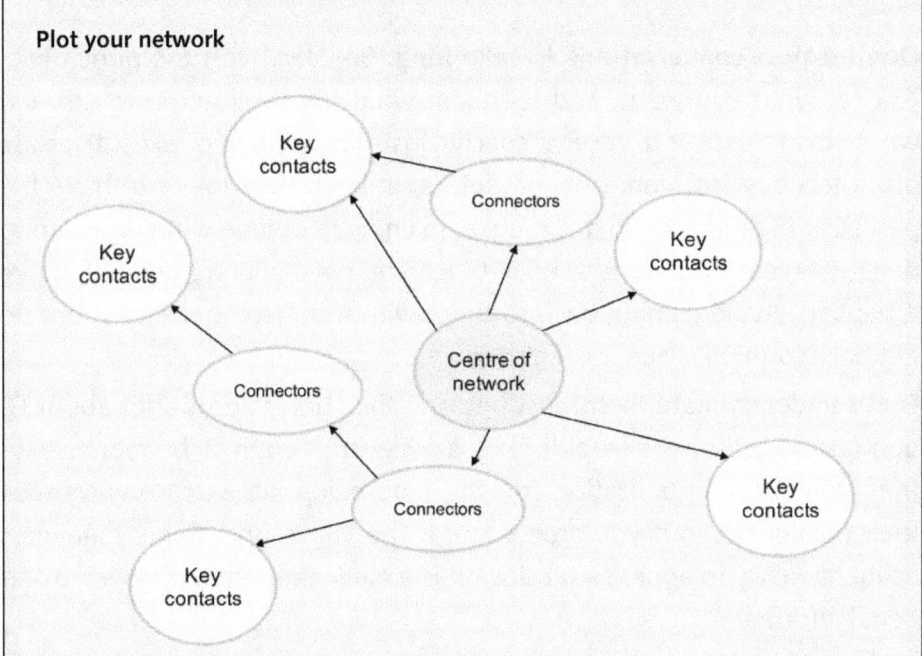

Plot your network

In putting your plan together, it is helpful to take a leaf out of the salesperson's book. The technique called "strategic selling" describes the importance of identifying key players and putting together an action plan to build influence. Use the five-step process below to identify key players who should be in your network of influence and build links to them.

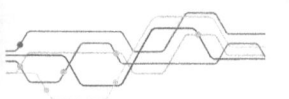

1. Go through your address book, and choose thirty contacts you know reasonably well in different parts of your organization.

2. Link them together in a network diagram format showing how they connect to you and other managers (as demonstrated above).

3. Add five other influential managers who you want to get to know better.

4. Identify the key connectors who connect them to you.

5. Put a plan together to get introduced to them (make sure you have something to talk about when you meet).

FIGURE 5. PLOT YOUR NETWORK

Don't expect conversations to take long. So, start with the punch line. Ask for what you want, and tell them what they will get in return and when. Don't expect to receive specific instructions. Senior executives are often too busy to work out the details; indeed, they may not have the particular expertise to do it. Often, explaining in outline what you plan to do is just what they want to hear. Once you have your agreement, make it happen. Avoid coming back to them with too many questions, but do get back to them when it is finished.

Don't underestimate them. Just because they don't know a lot about IT, don't assume they are stupid! They are clever enough to be more senior than you in the organization (for the time being, at least.) Always seek their opinion, even if you aren't sure if they have one. Some managers deliberately try to appear a bit slow. It is a tactic that often uncovers additional information.

Don't expect them to be warm and cuddly. Don't take abuse personally; it is one of the unfortunate facts of our hectic, e-mail-centric lives that senior managers can often be very curt, which can, in turn, appear rude. Even so, treat all managers with respect. Be confident—it is important that you speak regularly to senior managers and feel comfortable in their presence. Hang onto your sense of humor, but don't necessarily force it on others. What may be amusing to you may not be to them.

4.3 BUILDING YOUR NETWORK

To repeat our earlier claim, senior executives estimate that they spend up to 50 percent of their time networking! Of course, this does not mean they walk the corridors aimlessly, hoping to meet someone important to chat with. They see networking opportunities in their day-to-day work— in a project review meeting, say, or preparing a negotiation or at the start of a board meeting. They will not typically sit on their own in the coffee shop until the meeting was about to start, or eat a sandwich at their desk. They would be out and about, meeting with their network contacts, finding out about the changing priorities of the business, and sharing their views (influencing, if you like) on developments in IT.

To do this, you need a good network to work with. Networks do not just happen by accident. They require careful planning. Studies show that effective networks have good contacts at three levels of influence. The first circle includes your closest advisors and confidantes. It probably includes your direct reports and your boss, amongst others. You trust these people implicitly and would discuss with them any problems that were troubling you. The second circle of influence includes those people with whom you work regularly, and you probably know quite a lot about each of them. It is the third circle, though, that is the most interesting.

The third circle of influence contains those people who you see from time to time. You meet them perhaps every four to six weeks, sometimes less. They will almost always work in different departments that you don't come into contact with that often. This group will often include the senior executives and sponsors who are the most influential in the work you are doing, and will usually include your boss's boss. Unless you are on the board of directors, this group probably includes the CEO. The research consistently shows that it is this third group that holds the key for successful networkers.

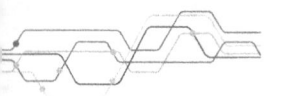
THE IMPORTANCE OF NETWORKS: HOW IBM WAS TRANSFORMED

It started in 1994. IBM was the official technology sponsor of the Lillehammer Winter Olympics in Norway. But when David Grossman, a mid-level IBM manager, tried to find the Olympic results website, he found a rogue website run by Sun, using IBM's raw data feed. Eventually IBM succeeded in shutting down the site. But the big problem was IBM's lack of awareness of what was going on in the new world of the Internet.

After the Olympics, Grossman drove to IBM's headquarters at Armonk. He hooked up a connection and showed IBM's head of marketing and a member of the strategy task force, John Patrick, what the Internet could do. From that point, Grossman was able to start an underground movement, mentored by Patrick. Patrick used his powerful network of contacts to open a lot of doors and build supporters, which soon included CEO Lou Gerstner. It was a classic case of the power of people networks to promote innovation and create energy for new ideas. It was the start of the revolution that enabled the Internet to become the major strategic thrust for the biggest computer company in the world.

From "Waking up IBM: How a gang of unlikely rebels transformed IBM," by Gary Hamel. To download the full article, to go to http://explore.hbr.org.

Studies show that communication around an organization often passes through a small number of people. These are the key business networkers, sometimes called "connectors," the people whom everyone knows. Set yourself the target of becoming one of the networkers within your organization. There is no more certain way to ensure career success than a good network of contacts. [17]

At this point, it might be helpful to map your network to see if you are focusing too much on your first two circles of influence. Of course, it is not

---

17   Malcolm Gladwell, *The Tipping Point*, (2001).

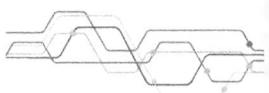
practical to drop everything to build influence further afield. Nonetheless, it can be really valuable to meet with them when the opportunity arises. One thing we have noticed is that people with valuable networks invest time to keep in touch.

Here are seven guidelines for building effective networks:

1. Choose your friends—identify the people you need to know and gravitate toward people with energy, ideas, and humor. Avoid people who are always complaining and resistant to change. Remember, you can tell a lot about people by the company they keep.

2. Faire le point—in France, managers arrange to meet their peers and other senior managers on a regular basis. "Faire le point" translates roughly as a "regular catch-up." These meetings typically take fewer than thirty minutes. They have no formal agenda— just the intention of catching up with what is going on.

3. Be in the right places at the right time, often known as "being visible."

4. Seek out opportunities for interaction, work closely with your boss, and build from his or her network.

5. Look for links with those you know in order to meet new people.

6. Get outside your comfort zone, and take calculated risks.

7. Seek to join the inner sanctum. This is the group of three or four people at the heart of any organization that holds the balance of power.

4.4 BE INFLUENTIAL

4.4.1 How Decisions Are Made

Peer leadership is about influencing decisions made that concern the interests of many different parties. So we should think carefully about how decisions are made. Generally, decisions are about choosing the best option that meets a number of criteria. Each criterion will typically have a different level of importance, and different options are measured against this weighting.. Logically, there are three areas where you can help. You can identify new criteria which may affect the decision; change the weighting of those criteria in the minds of the decision makers (of

which you may be one); or increase the number of options that are being considered.

Decisions are often made not based on facts, but on judgments, perceptions, and even prejudices. This isn't necessarily a problem. The point here is that you need to understand the priorities of your peers and colleagues. You need to understand the basis that they are using to make their decisions. When salesmen do their strategic sales analyses, they review all of the key decision makers and look at their motivations and decision criteria. IT managers need to do the same—understand the priorities of each key decision maker. Specifically, when doing your evaluation, think of the following:

1. What are the objectives of the other departments?

2. Who are the key players?

3. What are their motivations and behaviors?

4. What are the biggest influences they currently have? (In terms of people they know, projects they run, and so on.)

Think carefully as to what the decision makers will gain personally from a decision (for example, less work, less hassle, personal glory, and so on), and what their department will gain from the decision (more revenue or profitability, a better way of working for staff, or improved customer satisfaction). Then match your offering to the requirements of those decision makers.

4.4.2 Use Different Styles for Different Executives

Psychologists are generally in agreement that people are born differently. Everyone sees the world and make decisions in different ways. This might seem like an obvious statement, but it has important ramifications. When I was first introduced to the theory, I still held onto the belief that everyone basically thought the way I do, and their outlook was only slightly different because of their past experience. I thought that if they radically disagreed with me, they were either stupid or just being awkward. Of course, this is fundamentally not the case!

This it is very important for technical people to understand. The personality type of 60 percent of IT managers is such that they will tend

to see the detail in situations. They will make their decisions based on factual information. In contrast, 70 percent of CEOs do not see the detail in situations, unless it is clearly presented. They have a summary view of the world—not because they are doing a different job (although this has some influence), but because they see the world differently. Similarly, a high percentage of marketing directors will make decisions based not just on the facts, but on intangible factors. These decisions, which are often instinctive, are a complete anathema to many IT people.

So, in short, present to your audience in their preferred style. Tips are shown in table 12.

	Where you might find them	How to attract their attention	How to annoy them
Logical and structured	Accountants, IT professionals, sales managers	Structured, accurate, to-the-point presentations. Clear logical basis for findings and support material, if required.	Lots of detail that isn't relevant. Mistakes, such as adding errors. Illogical statements. Woolly and unstructured thoughts.
High-level thinkers	CEOs, lawyers, sales managers	High-level presentation in what is called an inductive or "pyramid" style. Start at the top level with logical layers of detail below, if required. Logical business models. Start with the summary.	Detailed and drawn-out presentations. Too much information. Keeping slides back; showing one bullet at a time.
Creative	Marketing directors	Creative imagery, out-of-the-box thinking, clear vision.	Being ungracious and impatient. Too many facts and data.
Friendly	HR managers	One-on-one discussions talking about specific situations in the here and now. Showing consideration for individuals in the company.	Being ungracious and impatient. Getting down to business without first taking the time to build a relationship.

TABLE 12. CHOOSING THE RIGHT INFLUENCING STYLE

Our ability to build relationships and influence across our organization is at the heart of this. You need to adjust your approach according to the window that your audience looks through. For example, do not try to give lots of detail to a CEO, who sees the world in summary. Use pictures, impressions, and imagery to influence a typical marketing director.

Five Rules for Presenting IT to Senior Executives
1. Be strategic, with a clear message and presentation logic.. Ask for what you want at the beginning. Your presentation may be cut short for any number of reasons.
2. Make any slide presentation short and sharp and the visuals clear and concise. During your preparation, keep asking yourself if something is relevant, and if it isn't, take it out. Too much detail makes it more likely you will get sidetracked. Make sure all your numbers are accurate and add up correctly.
3. Practice, practice, and then practice some more. You should be able to give your presentation without slides. Practicing is a great way to test whether your presentation has a clear thread. Ask a colleague to play the devil's advocate.
4. Let them learn what they should know or have forgotten. For example, if you are asking for $500K for an upgrade from version 7 to version 8 of the CCBS, you need to remind the audience what the CCBS is and how the business will benefit from the upgrade. Don't leave half the audience wondering if they should pluck up the courage to ask what it means (customer care and billing system as it happens!).
5. Stay alert. Don't lecture and don't start off brief and then go verbose. Aim to complete your presentation in half the allotted time and use the rest of the time for questions. Most of your audience will have read ahead anyhow, so don't keep them waiting, and encourage them to express their views.

TABLE 13. FIVE RULES FOR PRESENTING TO SENIOR EXECUTIVES

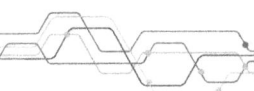

4.5 WHEN INFLUENCE TURNS TO POWER AND POLITICS

4.5.1 Identifying when Political Situations are Brewing

It is worth mentioning political awareness at this point. Building good networks is about growing your influence, both inside and outside of your organization. It is about making life unfair in your favor. But this can sometimes be misconstrued as being devious. When we ask delegates what words come to mind when they think of company politics, we often get words like *manipulative*, *secretive*, and so on. But this is misleading. Politics can have a very positive aspect.

Politics is defined as the process by which groups of people make collective decisions. In practical terms, this is the art of making decisions, where not everyone has the same end goals in mind. Decisions are therefore made based on influence and power. Of course, by their nature, collective decisions and actions will not suit everyone. And hence, there can be a temptation for some parties to use underhanded methods to get what they want. Understanding these currents is essential to good political management.

In fact, there are two factors when it comes to politics. First of all, being effective at politics requires presence and influence, as we have already discussed. The second factor is how this influence or power is used. The first rule of corporate politics states that whoever has the most power, always wins—except it is not always obvious where the power lies. It is a complex combination of different factors as shown in figure 6.

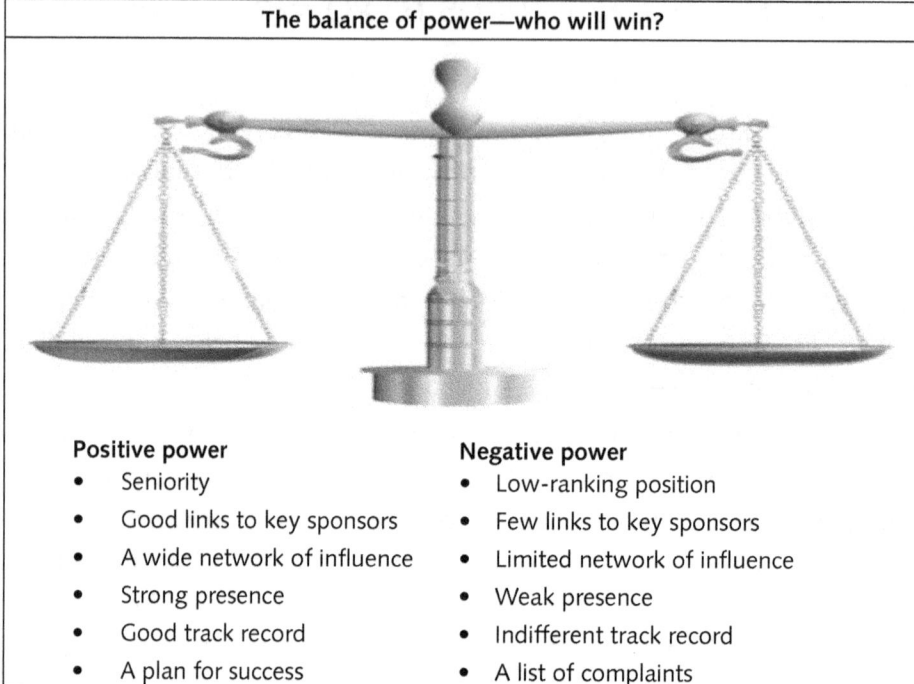

The balance of power—who will win?	
Positive power	**Negative power**
• Seniority	• Low-ranking position
• Good links to key sponsors	• Few links to key sponsors
• A wide network of influence	• Limited network of influence
• Strong presence	• Weak presence
• Good track record	• Indifferent track record
• A plan for success	• A list of complaints

FIGURE 6. THE BALANCE OF POWER

Let us not be naïve here. To be successful in managing your network and influence, you need to understand the political currents within your organization. There are many situations that generate strong internal political currents. To be effective, you need to be able to recognize them. Examples include under-pressure and under-performing managers; company acquisitions and mergers; two departments at odds; corporate programs (projects); and budget and investment planning.

4.5.2 Be Streetwise

In trying to chart the difficult waters of business, some managers will play games to try and gain an advantage. I do not recommend this as a long-term strategy. Game players invariably get found out and end up having to move on. Nonetheless, it is a fact of business life. For this reason, it can be helpful to know some of the tactics that they use so you can avoid

being caught out. Here is a list of a few examples we have come across. I am sure you have some of your own.

Take your opportunities. There are some decisions that senior managers just find too difficult to make and often delay. Politically aware managers have a sense as to when the right time is. As a technology manager, you will invariably have come across some examples of this, perhaps where the finance approval committee has held off on an infrastructure investment. So, in this case, a good time to resubmit a request might be shortly after the next outage. Just try to avoid looking smug.

CAROLINE'S STORY: WHAT HAPPENED THERE?

Someone was telling me about how teachers handle problems in the playground. If children (normally boys) are creating a nuisance, experienced teachers will not tell them to stop it. Instead, they will try to join in, and they take the steam out of the situation that way. When I was told this, I was reminded of a situation at work. One department did not want to pursue a particular project. They assigned someone from their own department to join the project. Whether purposefully or not, this person subtly but persistently undermined the project, by being helpful in an unhelpful way. In time, the project eventually stalled. At the time, I thought nothing of it, but looking back, maybe things weren't as innocent as I had first imagined.

Avoid bogus "development opportunities." Be wary if someone offers you a chance to work on a project that sounds too good to be true, offering great promises of career enhancement, gold bullion, and the like. Development opportunities, even difficult ones, are to be welcomed. But if you are being offered an opportunity where the previous incumbent was not successful, it is vital that you find out why, and gain any necessary commitments in terms of budget, resources, and management support. In summary, do not accept new assignments blindly.

Don't be bullied. Coercing people is forcing them to make a decision that they might not otherwise make. An example might be right before an important meeting, where one manager threatens the interests of another unless he or she is supported. Another more subtle form is name dropping—mentioning the name of someone senior who supports you and suggesting this person will be unimpressed if the other person does not support you as well.

4.6 DOS AND DON'TS FOR MANAGING SENIOR EXECS

By way of conclusion, here is a summary of some dos and don'ts.

Do:

- cultivate players who can build your leverage.
- build your "page rank" around the company with more links.
- develop future players.
- use your position as an IT manager at the heart of the business.
- be smart and make things work in your favor.
- act with integrity.

Don't:

- ignore the balance of power.
- play against someone more powerful than you.
- think you are invincible.
- spend too much time in your own work group.
- focus only on immediate results.

5. Assume Small Players have No Influence.

5.1 IN CONCLUSION

5.1.1 Leadership Opportunities

Here, we list some leadership opportunities that will help you get ahead in your career. Always look to develop your skills, and seek the guidance of your manager or a mentor. Management is a bit like golf. It needs good instruction and regular practice, or you will develop bad habits.

Leadership opportunities come to everyone—but not everyone recognizes them for what they are. Only those who are smart will recognize and take advantage of them. But if you really want to get ahead, you will need to create your own as well.

5.1.2 Personal Leadership

Personal strengths and weaknesses. It is important to know your strengths and weaknesses. Ask your manager, take a 360-degree survey or psychometric test, or use the assessment in *Strengths Finder*.

IT managers network. Become part of a professional group. Examples can include IT directors' forums and industry and professional associations. Other options include online social networking groups such as LinkedIn and our IT Leaders forum.

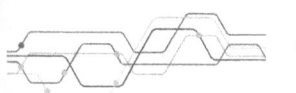
Industry profile. Successful IT professionals often have a high profile outside of their own organization. Look for opportunities to raise your profile at industry conferences, seminars, and other events. Build a reputation for yourself in an area of expertise, and think about writing a technical paper, either for publication in a major IT journal or internally (or both). Ask your PR department for advice. All the CIOs we interviewed were involved in charity work; examples include the *Computer Weekly* IT "sleep-out" event in support of the homeless and recycling old computers for third-world educational markets.

Network of suppliers. It is vital for all IT managers to build their network of contacts outside their peer group of IT managers. Take the opportunity to join senior-level briefings from your major technology providers. Get to know the major recruitment firms of IT managers—find the ten most influential firms responsible for recruiting the most senior posts. A number of them offer breakfast meetings where you get the chance to meet other IT directors.

Sources of learning. All senior IT managers have a thirst for knowledge. Think about your own sources of learning. These should include business journals as well as IT publications. The *Financial Times*, the *New York Times*, and the *Economist* provide high-quality sources on both business and technical developments. Look to journals such as *CIO* magazine, *Computer Weekly,* or *Computing*; technical reference sites and Internet blogs; or information providers, such as Gartner Inc. IT management and leadership courses provide a great opportunity for skills development and networking. Think about how you can build your knowledge of your own company, as well. Put the reporting dates of the quarterly financial results in your calendar, and take time to study new financial reports as they are issued. You should always have the most up-to-date facts and figures about your organization in your head.

5.1.3 Leadership Opportunities in Managing IT Teams

There are many possible leadership opportunities in the area of team leadership. Here are some ideas to get you started.

Change the environment. The environment in which your team works plays an important role in their productivity. It is easy to think that the environment cannot be changed, but there are many things that you can

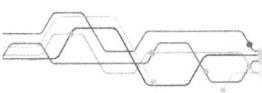

do to improve conditions within your building. This may require some investment—for example, new furniture, carpets, or pictures—but you may also be able to improve conditions through simple maintenance activities that reduce clutter and noise levels.

Performance monitoring. Start with the top-level company objectives and the departmental IT objectives. Set individual SMART objectives that have a line of sight to the top level objectives. Set standard targets and stretch targets. Review them regularly.

Induction and Training. Think about how new employees are looked after when they join the company. Do they have a manager and/or mentor assigned to show them how things work? Are they enrolled into the key company orientation programs? Is there an orientation program for IT, which explains the department's strategy and its key business processes, such as project life-cycles and operations?

Coaching. You will have many opportunities for coaching your staff. These may include team meetings or inter-departmental meetings. Work with your reports to make sure that they are fully briefed, and identify two or three coaching points that they should focus on when the meeting takes place. Remember the coaching role will depend on the team member. Less-experienced staff will need more specific guidance; experienced team members should be guiding the discussion and identifying their own points of priority.

Motivation. As the team manager, you have the responsibility of maintaining the motivational levels of your staff. This can take many forms—dinner or evening entertainment, for example, or an off-site seminar or conference. Ensure that these are properly planned. It is easy for motivational sessions to become counter-productive because of poor planning. One IT team organized a "treasure hunt" around London (using a similar idea to the film National Treasure starring Nicholas Cage where clues were arranged at different locations) for the company, providing an excellent opportunity to meet peers across the organization.

Team meetings. Team meetings offer an excellent opportunity for building rapport. One option is to plan your own workshop—asking someone

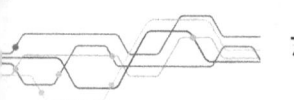

on your own team to share his or her knowledge with other team members on, say, a new technology or corporate program. Another opportunity for IT team meetings is to host a "technology showcase"—inviting in key vendors to ask them about technology futures, roadmaps, and advances that are being implemented in peer (competitor) organizations.

5.1.4 Leadership Opportunities in Business Relationship Management

Business relationship management offers the greatest opportunity for career enhancement.

Create a network plan. Use the techniques described in chapter 4 to identify your existing contacts and highlight new key contacts you need to get to know better. Look for opportunities to build bridges with them, such as helping them to resolve problems or working on common projects.

Faire le point. The French have an expression called "faire le point," which literally means to make the point. It refers to the short (typically 15 minutes) but regular meetings (typically every two weeks) that senior managers have with each other. You do not necessarily need a specific agenda, just a mutual agreement to share information and talk about new developments and opportunities.

Manage by opportunity. Be on the lookout for situations that make it easier to get difficult things done. For example, if the company finds it difficult to invest in backup hardware, use system downtime to emphasize the risks to the business of not having a backup plan in place.

Keep up to date. Keep up to date with the priorities of every department, and take every opportunity to build relationships with the heads of other departments. Invite the other department heads or leading technical experts to your regular management meetings.

Business travel. If you are traveling on business, identify if any other work colleagues or peers are also traveling to the same location, and take the opportunity to go out for lunch.

5.2 AND FINALLY

Take time to reflect

Within this book, we covered a lot of ground quickly. Depending on your current role, company, or situation, some ideas will be more relevant than others.

Next steps

Based on this review, you will identify many ideas about how to improve your performance. Think carefully about your own personal career development and that of your team. Identify a starting place, considering which ideas would have a significant impact on performance and be easy to implement. Then make a simple to-do list with deadlines for completion.

Staying ahead

Finally, the fact that you have taken time to read and think hard about the ideas presented here suggests that you are already a professional in your chosen discipline. However, all areas of business leadership are changing rapidly, and you should always to take steps to stay ahead as a leader in your field. If you found this book valuable, let us know. Other books in the series include

Book 2 - IT Strategy and Technology Innovation

Book 3 - Managing IT Projects and Leading Change

Book 4 - Business Management and Operational Performance

Good luck!

5.3 ABOUT THE AUTHOR

David McKean is a former CIO who has worked for several multinational companies around the world, including AT&T Ventures in Asia; UPC Nederland in Holland; and C&W UK. He is now the managing director of IT Leaders Ltd., a leading provider of IT management training programs.

In 1994, David joined Cable & Wireless as the program director for the third GSM license in France, securing one of the most profitable license wins for Cable & Wireless. Since that time, he has worked for several

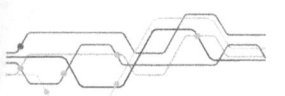

international blue-chip companies in Russia, France, Asia, and Holland, running large strategy development and business change programs. In Indonesia, in particular, he worked closely with all parts of the culturally diverse organization to build a business strategy that would meet the business priorities of all the different stakeholders. It was this work that led him to recognize the real difficulties that companies have in understanding a clear process for strategy; providing a rigorous and smart strategy; and then having to communicate it to different communities.

David is a regular conference presenter in Europe and Asia on strategy and technology leadership. He is a chartered engineer and a graduate of the University of Cambridge.

David McKean

IT Leaders, Greenlands, Henley-on-Thames, Oxfordshire, RG9 3AU, UK

E-mail: david.mckean@itleaders.co.uk; Telephone: 00 44 (0) 1491 57 86 88